A Crimson Tide

Poetry by Lena Kovadlo

A Crimson Tide - Copyright © 2012 by Lena Kovadlo

Book cover - Copyright © 2012 by Lena Kovadlo

All of the material contained in this book is the original work of the author.

No part of this book may be used or reproduced, stored in a retrieval system, or transmitted in any way or form or by any means electronic, mechanical, recording, or otherwise without the written permission of the author.

Published 2012 by Lulu Press
3101 Hillsborough St.
Raleigh, NC 27607

Printed in the United States of America
All rights reserved.

ISBN: 978-1-300-48358-8

Books by Lena Kovadlo

- *Pieces of Me*
- *Soundtrack of My Life: Volume 1*
- *Soundtrack of My Life: Volume 2*
- *Diary of a Crush*
- *Treasure*
- *Melodies of the Heart*
- *A Crimson Tide*

I'd like to thank everyone who has ever believed in me, encouraged me, inspired me, and supported me on my writing and publishing journey.

James L. Finley, Regis Auffray, Nicola Ward, Susan Joyner-Stumpf – you are my biggest fans and the greatest friends ever. Thank you for being a special part of my life and for making me a special part of yours. I love you guys!!!

Table of Contents

NATURE'S BEAUTIFUL PALATE ... 10

MOTHER NATURE ... 11
PRESENCE OF OUR MOTHERS ... 12
CLOUDS ... 13
SNOWY DAYS ... 14
THE MOON ... 15
THE SUN ... 16
CHANGE OF THE SEASON ... 17
BUSY BEE ... 18
LOST INSIDE THE DARKNESS ... 19
COMFORTED BY THE COLD ... 20
FAINT STROKES ... 21
WHITE ROSE ... 22

RED STROKES OF LOVE ... 23

WORDS LEFT UNSPOKEN ... 24
RED STROKES ... 25
IS OUR LOVE THE SAME ... 26
ON WINGS OF LOVE ... 27
HAUNTING ME AT EVERY TURN ... 28
GONE FOR GOOD ... 29
TO YOU I AM THE PAST ... 30
BARE YOURSELF TO ME ... 31
MY UNCARING FRIEND ... 32
WHY CAN'T I MEET SOMEONE WHO FEELS THE SAME ... 33
WANT TO BE SOAKED BY THE RAIN ... 34
LIFETIME WORTH OF MEMORIES GONE ... 35
ALL I'M LEFT WITH IS NOTHING ... 36
NOWHERE LEFT TO GO ... 37
LEFT WITHOUT A VALENTINE ... 38

A Crimson Tide | Poetry by Lena Kovadlo

YOU GAVE UP ON US	39
BECOMING A MEMORY	40
YOU ARE THE ONLY ONE	41
IMPRISONED BY DISTANCE	42
THE ONE	43
BITTERSWEET THOUGHTS	44
THE WEDDING	46
TWO A.M. (UNFORGETTABLE)	48
I CAN'T WAIT	50
PROMISE ME	51
LET US BE ONE	52
YOU UNBREAK MY HEART	53
I YEARN	54
MEANT TO BE	55
MORE THAN MY HEART CAN TAKE	56
WILL YOU FEEL THE SAME	57
THE ONE I WANT IS YOU	58
OCEANS OF YOUR LOVE	59
WISH YOU WERE HERE	60
YOU AND I MAKE A WHOLE	61
YOU HAVE SET ME FREE	62
A STRANGER	63
POURING OUT	64
TOO LATE TO MAKE YOU STAY	65
I WANT YOU HERE	66
CAN I?	67
A FATHER'S DEPARTURE	68
FRIENDS	69
YOUR WORDS, YOUR CHARM, YOUR LOVE	70
YOUR EYES AND YOUR SMILE	71
LOVE	72
YOU AREN'T REAL	73
TELL ME	74
YOUR LAUGH	75
FIGHTING FOR LOVE	76
I FEEL AND WISH	78
CRUSHED	79
TEXTING OVER CALLING	80
ETERNAL GOOD-BYE	81

A Crimson Tide | Poetry by Lena Kovadlo

HIDDEN	82
THE PRICE OF TRUE LOVE	83
THE KEY	84
CARRY ME	85
YOUR ANGELIC VOICE	86
BENEATH THE WEEPING WILLOW	87
THE WORDS (REGIS ACROSTIC)	88
LOVE ME FOR ME	89
YOUR PICTURE	90
REQUEST TO THE SUN	91
COME BACK	92
ADDICTION	93
VIVID DREAM	94
YOU ARE	95
YOU AND I IN THE ROUGH	96
YOUR LETTERS FROM THE SEA	100
ALONE TRYING TO FIND	101
CAN'T STAND THESE TWO	102
EVERYWHERE	103
ONE ENTITY	104
DAYDREAMING PRINCESS	105
SOMETHING THAT WILL NEVER BE	106
POLINA BRANDIS ACROSTIC	107
UNWANTED REALITY	108
FRIENDSHIP	109
HIDDEN INSIDE MY TREASURE	110
MY SOUL EXPOSED	111
VANISHED	112
WHERE WOULD I BE WITHOUT YOU?	113
DROWN IN DREAMS OF YOU	114
CLOSE IN OUR DREAM	115
RIGHT HERE FOR YOU	116
WITH YOU ON MY MIND	117
MISS YOU MY CURE	118
ALL THAT YOU DREAM	119
I'LL BE WITH YOU	120
BLOCKED	121
AUTOGRAPH POEM	122
YOU ARE THE SONG, YOU ARE THE FIRE	123

A Crimson Tide | Poetry by Lena Kovadlo

TO DREAM OF YOU 124
YOU ARE 125
MOUTHWATERING DELIGHT 126
MY WORDS 127
MELODIC EMBRACE 128
HEAVENLY LOVE 129
DON'T GIVE UP 130
WAITING 131

THE BLACK VEIL 132

LAID TO REST 133
HE LAY THERE ON DISPLAY 134
HIS OTHER HALF 135
IT'S TIME FOR YOU TO LEARN HOW TO DRIVE 136
THE POND 138
HEART FILLED WITH ARIAS 140
MY FINAL GOOD-BYE 142
NOWHERE TO BE FOUND 143
YOUR PRESENCE TAKING ME APART 144
ETERNAL SLUMBER 145
LEFT US 146
MEMORIES 147
NO LONGER HERE 148
YOUR BROTHER 149
DAY OF REMEMBRANCE 150

DARKENING THE PALE 151

EMBRACED BY THE DARKNESS 152
CAN'T GO BACK TO THE PAST 153
BITTERNESS 154
THE MIRROR 155
THE LAST TO KNOW 156
WAITING TO BE RELEASED 157

A Crimson Tide | Poetry by Lena Kovadlo

I'M A STRANGER	158
FROZEN HEART	159
TRAPPED IN THE CELL	160
IT ALL SEEMS LIKE A DREAM	161
A SCARED CHILD LIVES WITHIN	162
DREAM I YEARN FOR IN MY MIND	163
FEAR	164
TRYING TO MAKE THE FERRY	165
WHAT THE MIRROR ALWAYS SAYS	166
I AM A FLOWER	168
THE TREE	169
SAFE	170
COUCH POTATO	171
INVISIBLE PUPPY	172
TAKEN AWAY	173
A DREAM OR NOT?	174
IN THIS PLACE	176
UNCONTROLLABLE FEAR	177
WANDERING WOUNDS	178
THE WORDS	179
MISSING PIECES	180
ALIVE BUT DEAD	181
NORMAL OR NOT	182
NEVER-ENDING TAPE	183
IMMUNE	184
LONELY PAPER	186
LOST	187
THIS DIMENSION	188
NOTHING MATTERS	190
DECISIONS	192
MIDNIGHT SCREAMS	193
HAUNTING ME	194
A CHEATER'S HEART	195
TRAPPED WITHIN I SURRENDER	196
I'M A MISTAKE	197
I'M NOT A DOG	198
I AM A RIVER	199

NATURE'S BEAUTIFUL PALATE

There's nothing quite like being surrounded by the beauty and intrigue of Mother Nature. It is exhilarating and refreshing. It takes me away from reality, lets me escape from all of the worries and problems upon me, and makes me relax and unwind. And even when Mother Nature attacks us in an unpleasant or deadly way, it makes things interesting and more adventurous...

Not only do I love being surrounded by Mother Nature but I also enjoy writing about it a great deal. So in this section you will find poetry dedicated to Mother Nature...

~ MOTHER NATURE ~
September 1, 2012

I want nature to surround me
    With its majestic beauty
        With every passing day
            That comes to me

        I will embrace it
    Welcome it
        With arms open wide

    For there is nothing better
  Nothing more unique
Than Mother Nature

~ PRESENCE OF OUR MOTHERS ~
August 23, 2011

The morning breeze
Like a mother's touch
Embraces me with comfort
The birds' echoing song
Like an angelic lullaby
Wafts in the air
All reminders
That our mothers are always present
No matter where we are
Or what we do

~ CLOUDS ~
November 17, 2010

Brush strokes filled with shades of white
Glide across a baby blue canvas
Painting a mural for all to see

Let your imagination soar up to the heavens
And open your heart and soul
To the beauty and wonder
Of Mother Nature's artistic creation
That comes to life on this glorious day

~ SNOWY DAYS ~
February 10, 2010

Closing my eyes,
I dive into the fluffy goodness
And drift to a special place,
Where I am a kid again
Enjoying a life filled with wonder.

It is on these days
That the silence turns to a melody
I yearn to hear;
A melody that soothes my every core
And brings with it eternal peace.

~ THE MOON ~
April 10, 2010

A round ball of silver light
Hangs overhead this darkened night
Its shadow spreading all around
Where life once roamed now can't be found

~ THE SUN ~
April 6, 2010

A round ball of yellow light
Hangs up above where birds take flight
It warms the soul, brings the smiles
That last on faces all the while

~ CHANGE OF THE SEASON ~
April 2, 2010

The lonely tree, naked,
    Exposing bitter scars,
        Endured during nature's months of hibernation,
            Awakens once more
                With new life.

Harsh memories washed away
    By nature's tears,
        By nature's reawakening,
           As spring opens its vigorous arms,
              Covering everything with new life.

~ BUSY BEE ~
March 16, 2010

When the sun wakes,
      The busy bee flies to work,
            Spreading his seed
                  Wherever he lands.

                        When the sun goes to bed,
                  The busy bee flies home,
            His seeds blooming,
          Expanding into new life;
      A life that will give birth to another,
Until all around lives again.

~ LOST INSIDE THE DARKNESS ~
January 19, 2010

Awake at night,
The pale moonlight,
    It beckons me to fly away
    Into the darkness of the day.

    I'm lost inside the mystery,
    Rewriting bits of history;
The ones that faded with the day,
To make my future be okay.

A Crimson Tide | Poetry by Lena Kovadlo

~ COMFORTED BY THE COLD ~
January 19, 2010

A huggable puppy,
Red and white,
Sits beside me
On this cold night.

                    But I won't embrace it.
                    I welcome the cold;
                    It comforts me now
                    As my feelings unfold.

The puppy a gift,
A reminder of love,
That froze in time
When spring reigned above.

                    I don't want to be warmed
                    By the season that passed,
                    So I'll sit here alone,
                    With the cold and rest.

~ FAINT STROKES ~
January 30, 2009

The faint strokes of grayish blue

Illuminate earth's tidal tears

    As they rain down on nature's creations,

        Penetrating every molecular crevice of its children,

            Those that breathe the eternal life,

            And those whose breath has PAUSED forever.

~ WHITE ROSE ~
July 29, 2007

Your white rose
A glittering desire of snowflakes
Brushed with delicious love

A Crimson Tide | Poetry by Lena Kovadlo

RED STROKES OF LOVE

When love is in the air, it is incredible. You feel things you have never felt before; things that make it seem as if you are living in a fairy tale dream. It may even seem too good to be true, but it is real, very real.

Falling in love is the best feeling to experience. It is like a drug that you can't get enough of. We all go through it at some point, and when we do, it leaves a lasting imprint deep inside us that we will never forget.

Of course sometimes falling in love comes with a price, when the one you love chooses to go his/her own way, leaving you heartbroken, in tears, and sometimes scarred for life.

Poetry in this section is of course dedicated to love – the sweet, the bitter, and the dark – and all that comes along with it.

~ WORDS LEFT UNSPOKEN ~
October 26, 2012

There are words that are left unspoken
        There are words that are silenced for life
                There are words that will always be hidden
                      And will never reach you my love

                For there's fear reigning inside me
        For I've yet to be brave to speak up
And tell you I yearn for you baby
And tell you my feelings are strong

I don't want these words left unspoken
        I want to fight this battle and win
                Otherwise I'll forever be tormented
                      By the words left unspoken within

~ RED STROKES ~
October 24, 2012

Everywhere I turn

I see red strokes surround me

    Love blooms like the garden

    Hearts break like shattered glass

Red roses expanding

Their aroma uplifting

    Then suddenly every petal

    Withering, falling to the ground

Red strokes of love

Red strokes of heartbreak

    They are everywhere I turn

I've seen them

I've lived them

I can't escape them

    For without them

    There would be no life

~ IS OUR LOVE THE SAME ~
May 7, 2012

The love I feel for you is undying
A special love that burns from within
And feeds me with fuel I need to function

I love you real and true
And my heart says so do you
But is our love really the same
When you belong to another
And share a bond you and I never will

~ ON WINGS OF LOVE ~
May 2, 2012

You come to me on wings of love
Flying high over oceans wide
Landing atop my still beating heart
And it is there you will settle
Fluttering your angelic wings
For all eternity and beyond

~ HAUNTING ME AT EVERY TURN ~
April 13, 2012

My mind is filled with thoughts of you
Everywhere I turn you're there
Haunting me at every turn
Not letting me breathe
Or have a moment of tranquility
You have disappeared from my life
Without a warning
And yet here you are
Appearing before me
Laughing with your signature laugh
As if nothing is wrong
As if your presence is welcomed
Why can't you just let me be
And haunt someone else
I no longer wish you around

~ GONE FOR GOOD ~
April 13, 2012

After crossing paths in the virtual world
Facebook became our daily hangout
As we chatted for days on end

Though we were oceans apart
I felt the distance shrink between us
As if you and I were in the same room

But soon after you forgot my existence
And the distance increased between us
Leaving me swimming in oceans of blue

You were there still in our daily hangout
But you remained silent and cold
As if you and I never crossed paths

Oh how I wished for your name to disappear
For any trace of you to be erased
So I would no longer be swimming in oceans of blue

But when it finally happened
Those oceans of blue made me drown
Because it was then I knew you were gone for good

~ TO YOU I AM THE PAST ~
March 9, 2012

Forever your caring friend
These were the last words
That you laid upon me
Before you went on your way

Weeks have passed slowly
And you, my once caring friend
Have not one care in the world
When it concerns me

For your path no longer crosses with mine
But instead with another
Who you deem more important than me

To you I am nothing but the past
Nothing but forgotten memories
That can never resurface from their hiding place

Why then were your last words to me
Forever your caring friend
Was that your way of telling me
That all the events leading up to this moment
Never held any meaning beyond a dream

~ BARE YOURSELF TO ME ~
March 14, 2012

Stand beside my window bare
Showing me your tender care
Shower me with love unending
The real you with no pretending
I don't want to say good-bye
But will have to if you lie

~ MY UNCARING FRIEND ~
February 12, 2012

You say you're my caring friend
Yet where are you when I need you
How come you never say hello
Never ask me how I am doing
Never want to know about my life
Or what's roaming through my mind
Why are you so distant, so cold
You might as well not exist
Because you are not around anyway

~ WHY CAN'T I MEET SOMEONE WHO FEELS THE SAME ~
February 12, 2012

When I fall in love
They leave as fast as they arrive
When I feel no more than friendship
They stay with a smitten smile on their face
Why can't I meet someone
Where we're both in love
And want to be together forever
Without lies, games, or hidden agendas

~ WANT TO BE SOAKED BY THE RAIN ~
February 2, 2012

I want to
find myself
soaked by the
rain, the heavy
downpour cascading
down my body; merging
with the flooding of my heart
caused by the tsunami you brought
upon me when you chose to speed sail to a different place; to a place
where I am an imprint in the sand washed away by the tide;
where I am nothing but a mirage; where I am
a distant memory on the horizon.

~ LIFETIME WORTH OF MEMORIES GONE ~
February 2, 2012

We have kept in touch for only a few months
But it feels like we've been at it for years
And now that it's over
It feels like a lifetime worth of memories and dreams
Are no longer alive and burning bright
But instead are buried deep below the ground
That will never be reborn
No matter how much I try
To bring them back to life

~ ALL I'M LEFT WITH IS NOTHING ~
February 2, 2012

I've bared my heart, my soul, my flesh to you
And you've done the same
But then you left my heart bare too
Taking away all my hopes and dreams
All the love that burned for you
Taking away what I thought was real

I've bared myself to you in every way
And now all I'm left with is nothing
But a bitter taste in my mouth
Sour tears in my eyes
That fall like acid rain
Hollowness in my heart and soul
And a feeling that I am being eaten away
Slowly until there's nothing left of me to bare

~ NOWHERE LEFT TO GO ~
February 2, 2012

I was so sure my future with you
Was on the horizon
Was a clear path with no derailment
To the things I yearned for, for years
But never got to experience

I was so sure that you and I
Were on the train to the happiest moments,
To the most unforgettable experiences
To the memories that would last a lifetime

I was so sure we would travel together through life
Until there was nowhere left to go
Till we reached our final destination

I was so sure of my future
Of you and me and what we would become
As the clock kept ticking away

But what I thought had derailed
For you've taken the train to a different route
And you and me have reached a final destination
With nowhere left to go

~ LEFT WITHOUT A VALENTINE ~
February 2, 2012

My heart overflowed with happiness
Knowing that you would be my Valentine
But now it overflows with sorrow
Because you have vanished
And I am left without a Valentine
To call my own
To share this special moment of love with
And to create a lasting memory
That I'll savor for the rest of my life

~ YOU GAVE UP ON US ~
February 2, 2012

You gave up on us
        Even before we met
Even before we saw
        If the two of us together
Formed a link in the chain
        Were the missing piece of the puzzle
You gave up on us
        As if you and I don't matter
As if you and I are not meant to be

~ BECOMING A MEMORY ~
January 30, 2012

With every day that goes by
You are becoming a memory
A ghost of past existence

My future with you seems in the past
And our dreams become nothing but dreams

You say you haven't vanished
Then why are you nowhere to be found

~ YOU ARE THE ONLY ONE ~
January 30, 2012

Even with all the obstacles on the horizon
You are the only one
Who gave me a sense of belonging
Who talked about sharing a name
Who never gave up on me
On us
On our future
Who pictured us together forever

~ IMPRISONED BY DISTANCE ~
January 21, 2012

For so long I've waited for you
The one who would accept me for who I am
No strings attached
The one who would want to be with me forever
No ultimatums
No games or lies
The one who would love me deeply
And complete me in every way

At last I've found you my love
But though my feelings mimic your own
Though you are here with me
We are forever oceans apart
Forever being imprisoned by distance
Forever being torn apart

Only a miracle can save us
And bring us together at last

~ THE ONE ~
January 21, 2012

You appear in a place I least expected
A few months after I catch the bride's bouquet.
Though we have yet to meet,
Though we have yet to spend time together,
Deep down inside it feels so right.

You are the one I've been hoping to find.
And now that I have found you
I never want to let you go.
I want to be with you forever
Through every waking moment
And every moment of slumber.

I want to be with you forever,
Not just as a friend,
Not just as a lover,
But your dashing bride
And faithful wife.

I want to journey through life with you
Through every happiness
And every sorrow.
I want to share it all
For you are the one that was meant for me,
And I am the one that was meant for you.

~ BITTERSWEET THOUGHTS ~
January 21, 2012

I close my eyes to the night,
Hide under the covers of my bed,
And with glistening tears running down my face,
Let my thoughts drift away
Passed oceans wide,
And mountains deep,
Transporting me to the faraway lands
To your small, cozy palace.

I find you standing by the window,
Your hand touching the cold glass,
Looking out at the city life
That stretches out before you.
You have a faraway look in your eyes
And glistening tears running down your face.

I know that you are thinking of us
Together in your king sized bed
Locked in a warm passionate embrace,
Our lips entangled in the sweetest kisses,
Our two hearts and souls united as one.

Yet these thoughts are bittersweet
For we are both trapped in faraway lands
Imprisoned by vast fields,
Oceans wide,
Mountains deep.

A Crimson Tide | Poetry by Lena Kovadlo

Our union is yet to be real
But at least these thoughts
That, I too, have running through my head
Make me feel that you and I are real
And that what we have is real too.

It will just take a bit longer
Before the distance shifts
And our faraway lands merge together
Into one complete kingdom
In which you and I will reign
Not just as friends and lovers
But also as husband and wife.

A Crimson Tide | Poetry by Lena Kovadlo

~ THE WEDDING ~
January 21, 2012

Single girls huddle together
Their eyes on the beautiful bouquet
The bride holds in her hand.
The room is hushed
As the bride prepares for the throw.
The girls around me melt away
And my eyes lock with yours.

I know how the movie will play out.
I will catch the bouquet
So you will catch the garter,
And we will slow dance together
Like Cinderella and Prince Charming at a ball,
As everyone's eyes are glued on the two of us.

At last the bouquet flies through the air
Passed the hungry girls and into my arms.
I feign surprise and walk over to the chair
That's been waiting for me this whole time.
I sit down, lift up my leg
And let your hands glide up my dress
As you slide the garter as high as it can go.

Then you take your hands in mine
And lead me to the dance floor
Where it is only you and I
Lost in the magical moment
As the music floats through the quiet room.
We let the music take hold of us
And when I stumble
You are there to catch me from falling.

A Crimson Tide | Poetry by Lena Kovadlo

The whole night you are there
Locking your eyes with mine,
Letting our fingers intertwine,
And our bodies unite,
In one dance after another,
Until it is time for us to part.

I have caught the bouquet,
You have caught the garter,
And we have been united for the evening,
Perhaps even for the rest of our lives.
Yet, that was never going to be
Because you have chosen to forget my existence
And leave me there to stumble and fall
From an already broken heart.

~ TWO A.M. (UNFORGETTABLE) ~
January 21, 2012

It is two a.m. and the deafening silence
Is being broken by the echo
Of my fingers striking the dormant keys,
Filling the empty pages
With the words escaping like a bullet
From deep within my beating heart.

Though slumber falls upon me this night
My fingers won't let my thoughts drift
To the empty bed calling out to me,
Won't let my tired eyes droop
And surrender to the night.

Tonight, I am imprisoned
By the words of my heart
That have been locked up tight
And have now been set free.
It can only be you my love
That is keeping me here
Glued to the computer screen
As I type away into the night.

Others are having their adventures
Being lost in the land of dreams.
But I have an adventure of my own,
As I pour out my heart onto the empty pages
That will soon be filled
With memories I will never forget.

A Crimson Tide | Poetry by Lena Kovadlo

It is you who is here with me,
You who will keep me awake,
You who will make these memories
Unforgettable.

~ I CAN'T WAIT ~
January 21, 2012

I can't wait to taste your lips
To caress your fingertips
To dissolve in all your love
And to fly through skies above
I can't wait 'til you are mine
'Til you walk with me through time
Through the happiness and sorrow
Through the future of tomorrow

~ PROMISE ME ~
January 21, 2012

Promise me you won't surrender
That you won't give up this fight
Promise me that you'll have patience
That you'll wait 'til we unite
Promise me that you'll be faithful
'Til we're standing face to face
Promise me that from this moment
I'm the one you'll always chase

~ LET US BE ONE ~
January 21, 2012

Take my hand in yours so gentle,
And lead me to the throne that awaits us.
Let us drown under its white silky covers,
And unite in the passionate embrace,
As our bodies discover each other
Under the starry night that awakens.
Let us feed each other with a long awaited desire
That's been yearning to unfold.
Let us melt into each other tonight
And every night that follows us into the future.
Let us be what we were meant to be.
Let us be now and forever ONE.

~ YOU UNBREAK MY HEART ~
January 21, 2012

One broken heart after another
Sometimes I wonder why I bother
To lose myself inside the love
That leaves me here in the rough
That leads my heart to bleed and shatter
And makes me feel that I don't matter

But then you come into my life
And make the dead love come alive
And now I feel that I do matter
And that my heart won't bleed and shatter
'Cause you're the one that's meant for me
The one who'll always set me free
With you the love will always burn
And I will never see it torn

~ I YEARN ~
January 21, 2012

For the first time it feels so right
You and me together in flight
My heart yearns for us to unite
Together forever side by side
I yearn for love for your embrace
To wipe the tears from your face
I yearn for you to be my man
I yearn for you to take my hand
For only you can break the seal
And lead me through this love so real

~ MEANT TO BE ~
January 21, 2012

Far away and yet so near
You and me forever dear
I will love you deep and true
Now and always linked to you
And the love will only grow
Unlike any we have known
You and I are meant to be
Our souls will set us free

A Crimson Tide | Poetry by Lena Kovadlo

~ MORE THAN MY HEART CAN TAKE ~
January 11, 2012

I've long forgotten the tears
That spilled from my eyes like raging rivers
Whenever I thought of days without you
Or reminisced about the days we'd shared
I've long moved on from everything you meant to me
From what we were and what we'd been through
When you were present in my life

But now that I find you with another
Now that I find you on one bended knee
Asking her to share your future
And her saying *yes!* with overflowing happiness
As she kisses you with a sweet passion
The tears spill once more like raging rivers
And everything comes flooding back to me like a tsunami

I wish for her to be washed away with the tide
For you to be left standing on one bended knee
Proposing to thin air
Because having her there
Is more than my heart can take

~ WILL YOU FEEL THE SAME ~
January 5, 2012

We haven't even met
And yet your mind's been set
You want me here forever
For us to be together

We're soul mates you say
Forever we will stay
But will it all hold true
When I will meet with you

Will you feel the same way
And will you want to stay
Or will you choose to run
And leave me here alone

I hope you won't leave me
I hope you will stay
I feel you complete me
In every way

~ THE ONE I WANT IS YOU ~
January 5, 2012

Are you going to stick around
Or will you leave like all the rest
I don't want to hear this sound
And I'm hoping for the best
I am hoping you won't leave me
And that all you say is true
Understand and please believe me
That the one I want is you

A Crimson Tide | Poetry by Lena Kovadlo

~ OCEANS OF YOUR LOVE ~
January 1, 2012

I swim in the oceans of your love
Soothed by its gentle caress
As it washes over me
I taste every drop on my tongue
And yearn to dissolve in you
As the moon casts its shadow over the water
And the stars illuminate the night

~ WISH YOU WERE HERE ~
December 27, 2011

I wish you were here
Lying beside me
I wish you were here
To hold to touch
I wish you were here
To love and to cherish
I wish you were here
My dear so much

~ YOU AND I MAKE A WHOLE ~
November 7, 2011

I thought you belonged to me
That we were one entity
But my theory was never true
Because you are a part of another equation
One that doesn't include me
One that takes a part of you
And shares you with another
I never want to share you with another
Only you and I, alone, make a whole

~ YOU HAVE SET ME FREE ~
November 7, 2011

I take the open road
I don't know where it leads
But one thing is for certain
My heart no longer bleeds

I'm putting you behind me
As I go on my way
From this point on I promise
I won't waste a single day

You'll always be a memory
But you'll no longer be
The one that makes me suffer
For you have set me free

~ A STRANGER ~
November 7, 2011

I look through the thick crowd
Trying to find your silhouette
Leaning against the exit door.
My eyes shift
Left,
      Right,
Front,
      Back,
But your familiar frame
Is nowhere in sight.

I make my way to the center
And stand there unmoving,
Looking out at the terminal,
Now becoming empty,
Looking out at the starry night outside,
But I see only strangers.
Maybe you have become a stranger
And that's why you're nowhere to be found.

~ POURING OUT ~
September 19, 2011

I pour out my heart on paper
Filling the empty pages
With my every desire
My every hope and dream
Pouring out my feelings
For you and us and our union
For our future days ahead

I pour out all that I have
For you and only you alone
In hopes that when you
Drink up all that I've written
And let it soak inside you
That you will pour out your heart
Your every desire, hope and dream
On those empty pages
That you will tell me that I
Am a part of everything
You yearn to bring to life

~ TOO LATE TO MAKE YOU STAY ~
September 19, 2011

I panicked and pushed you away
But it's too late to make you stay
You have moved on to someone new
To love, to sleep with, marry too

~ I WANT YOU HERE ~
September 10, 2011

I want to run away with you into the night
I want to soar above the clouds like birds in flight
I want you near me night and day, an angel dear
Through every waking, sleepless moment want you here
And when I'm dreaming in the night I want you there
To be beside me, guide me through my dreams so fair

~ CAN I? ~
September 9, 2011

Can I carry you in my pocket
Maybe wear you around my neck
Can I place you in a locket
Lounge with you upon the deck
Can I be with you forever
Can I dream of you at night
Dance with you until forever
Until we both take our flight

~ A FATHER'S DEPARTURE ~
August 23, 2011

She stands by the airport window
Her hand on the cold, foggy glass
Watching her father
Get smaller and smaller
As he walks onto the plane
Tears start to run down her face
Knowing her father has left her
With a one-way ticket in his hand
Even her mother's soothing touch
Does nothing to comfort her
Even the presence of her mother
Will not bring her father back

~ FRIENDS ~
July 9, 2011

Many people come and go from our lives
Most we tend to forget
But there are those few
Who stand out
Who mean the world to us
Who hold a special place in our heart
They are dear friends
Friends we will cherish forever
Friends who will be with us
Through the good and the bad
Until we die

~ YOUR WORDS, YOUR CHARM, YOUR LOVE ~
Summer 2011

Your kind words will keep me warm
No matter what you'll be my charm
And I'll forever be entwined
By all your love – the sweetest wine

~ YOUR EYES AND YOUR SMILE ~
Summer 2011

Your eyes sparkle bright
Like the stars in the night
And your smile divine
Will forever be mine

~ LOVE ~
April 30, 2011

Learning the art
Of caring, sharing
Vowing to be there
Every time I fall

~ YOU AREN'T REAL ~
April 30, 2011

You say you love me
Say you'll be there when I need you
And while that comforts me
Inside I know the truth

Even though you love me
You'll never be there when I need you
Because you aren't real
You are just words on a computer screen

~ TELL ME ~
August 31, 2010

Look into my eyes and tell me
You'll never go away
Tell me that you'll never leave me
That you're here to stay

Tell me that your search is over
That you've found the one
Tell me I'm your girl forever
Tell me life's begun

Tell me all will be okay
Tell me that it's true
Tell me that from this fine day
It will be me and you

~ YOUR LAUGH ~
August 21, 2010

Your laugh is what I need
To get me through another day
Your laugh is what I need
To feel that all will be okay

Your laugh it lifts me up
It is my sunshine in the rain
Your laugh it warms me up
It takes away all of the pain

Your laugh it lives in me
And it will never go away
Your laugh it sets me free
And I am soaring through the day

Your laugh it is my laugh
It is our laugh, will always be
The medicine I'll always have
The one that sets me free

~ FIGHTING FOR LOVE ~
August 10, 2010

See you later darling
This is not good-bye
I will be returning
Back into your life

I am only leaving
Because I have no choice
Fighting for our freedom
For the right of voice

I am not a quitter
I will not back down
I will be returning
Once I've won the crown

Your love will keep me burning
It will keep me strong
Always deep inside me
Where it belongs

See you later darling
I'll be on my way
Let my love inside you
Never let it stray

I will never leave you
I won't say good-bye
You're the most important
Person in my life

A Crimson Tide | Poetry by Lena Kovadlo

You're what keeps me going
Every day and night
You're what gives me courage
To stand up and fight

For the love of freedom
For the right of voice
You and I forever
That's my only choice

Always and forever
You and I will be
Nothing is going stop me
When you're here with me

~ I FEEL AND WISH ~
May 20, 2010

When I look up at the stars
Shining above me in my room
I feel a connection to your soul
I feel your closeness, your touch
I feel that you and I are meant to be
And wish for the stars to unite us
So that when I look up at the stars
You are not some endless miles away
But instead right here lying beside me

~ CRUSHED ~
April 27, 2010

When the one that you love
Has walked out the door
    Your dreams are crushed
    And crushed even more
        When you find out
        He moved on ahead
To some other person
To love and to wed

A Crimson Tide | Poetry by Lena Kovadlo

~ TEXTING OVER CALLING ~
April 2, 2010

You type away on your cell phone
Sending me message after message
Knowing I'd rather hear your voice.
Why do you do that when all it takes
Is a press of a button to talk to me
Voice to voice,
Soul to soul,
Heart to heart.

~ ETERNAL GOOD-BYE ~
April 2, 2010

After a weekend having fun
He called her up and said *we're done!*
He didn't feel the same as she
And said that friends is all they'd be.
Now hands around her throat tight,
She says good-bye to vacant night.
The drowning tears, pools of red.
For her, tonight, true love is dead.

~ HIDDEN ~
March 16, 2010

Hidden under the covers,
Lies the diary of a crush.
Its pages once empty,
Are now filled with detailed accounts
Of bittersweet love.

It is on these pages of love
That her soul lives,
That her soul hides,
In hopes to save itself
From another heartache.

~ THE PRICE OF TRUE LOVE ~
March 16, 2010

Somewhere in this strange world of cyberspace
She met an incredible soul
Who brightened her days,
Made her smile,
Made her believe true love existed.
But this true love came with a price –
Distance and loneliness,
And a yearning for a union that can never be.

~ THE KEY ~
February 19, 2010

I gave you the key
To my soul, my heart.
You didn't embrace it,
Just tore it apart.

You left a big hole
Deep within me and more,
You were too blind to see
As you walked out the door.

Here I am now, alone,
Left with these open scars,
Left here silently battling
All these painful wars.

Inside of me,
Inside my soul,
Emotions broken,
I am out of control.

Give back my life,
Give back the key,
And let me live here,
Misery-free.

A Crimson Tide | Poetry by Lena Kovadlo

~ CARRY ME ~
February 14, 2010

Carry me through clouds,
Through raging seas and lands.
    Carry me through currents
    Of wind's caressing hands.
        Carry me through sunshine,
        Through rays of burning light.
        Carry me through moonlight
        That illuminates the night.
    Carry me through stars above
    Where dreams and magic hide.
Carry me through love forever
With you I yearn to ride.

~ YOUR ANGELIC VOICE ~
February 6, 2010

How I miss your angelic voice
That escapes from within you
Taking hold of me
Wrapping me in comfort
Warming me from head to toe

~ BENEATH THE WEEPING WILLOW ~
February 4, 2010

Beneath the weeping willow
I sit on a clear sunny day
Drifting back to the past
To the memories of love
That once roamed free
Wishing that at this moment
These memories of love
Were not just dreams
But present happenings
I get to savor on this day
Wishing that at this moment
You were here with me
Beneath the weeping willow
Bringing these memories back to life

~ THE WORDS (REGIS ACROSTIC) ~
February 2, 2010

Ripe are the words
Escaping your heart
Growing with sweetness
In batches of love
Spilling the fruits of your soul

~ LOVE ME FOR ME ~
January 19, 2010

Love me for the beauty that lies within,
Not for the beauty that makes your head spin.
Love me for me, for who I am inside,
No matter the picture I paint at night.
I'll do the same, I'll love you true
For the beauty that lies within you too.

~ YOUR PICTURE ~
January 19, 2010

When we were together,
I could not stop staring at your picture;
But now that you are no longer here,
I cannot stare at your picture anymore,
Not even for a moment,
Because that brings unending tears
And a stop to my heart.

~ REQUEST TO THE SUN ~
January 8, 2010

Oh sun!
Blind me with your scorching rays.
I do not want to see
The love burning before me.

The flame of love,
It is everywhere I turn,
Haunting me,
Blazing through me,
Opening up the wounds of my ashen heart.

I am scarred by every flicker of love surrounding me,
A love that is not my own.
I am begging you sun,
Blind me with your scorching rays
Until I have my own fiery love to ignite me.

~ COME BACK ~
December 9, 2009

Baby can you hear me crying in the rain
Baby can you feel my overflowing pain
Don't you see that I still love you
I just can't get enough of you
Please come back and dry my tears
Help erase these painful spheres
Do not leave, don't say good-bye
'Cause without you I will die

~ ADDICTION ~
December 9, 2009

He is wasted on the memories
He is drunk from love gone by
This love is an addiction
He cannot leave behind
Because he is still in love
With the one who left him blind

~ VIVID DREAM ~
December 8, 2009

I dream of you
The dream so vivid and real
Feels like you're right here with me
I feel your touch
See your smile and beautiful face
Hear your soothing voice
And it seems like we never parted
As if you and I are still one and the same
Still the couple I yearn for us to be

~ YOU ARE ~
October 21, 2009

You are the breath of freshest air
The drop of the refreshing rain
You are the snowflake on my tongue
With you I feel oh so alive

~ YOU AND I IN THE ROUGH ~
April 7, 2009

We were together for awhile.
Not sure what we were to each other,
But we were together
And that's all that mattered.

        We had some rough patches
        But through it all
        We were very close
        And nothing could tear us apart.

Then one day without a thought
I let my feelings slip,
Revealing how another made me feel
And how he felt for me.

        I always shared everything with you,
        My life, my soul, the inner me.
        I never thought you'd get mad,
        Say things that you'd never say.

But you did tell me these things.
You were angry, I was hurt.
I felt you wanted nothing
To do with me anymore.

A Crimson Tide | Poetry by Lena Kovadlo

I was afraid your dirty words
Would sting me again.
I told you to stop contacting me,
To stop sending me letters.

       You obeyed my orders,
       Vanishing from my life.
       I was sinking deep in emotion,
       Drowning with each passing day.

Not only were you no longer here,
But another who kept on repeating
How much he loved me,
Toyed with me and wounded me deeply,

       Deep to the point where
       I love you was something I feared.
       How do I know it's real?
       How do I trust these words ever again?

I don't want to fall into the trap
Of artificial love,
A love that will only die
And leave me wounded for life.

A Crimson Tide | Poetry by Lena Kovadlo

I regret falling for another,
Can't believe I ever did.
But it happened
And there is no way to change the past.

       I regret for letting you know,
       And letting you go,
       When all along
       The only person I truly loved was you.

Something made you take a chance
And write me a very short letter,
And that something brought us together
Again, stronger and best of friends.

       The past will forever live inside us
       And will haunt us into the future,
       But I know I love only you
       And you're the only one I'll ever truly love.

You're the best person in my life.
I cannot live in this world without you.
If you vanish from me again
Then I will vanish along with you.

A Crimson Tide | Poetry by Lena Kovadlo

I need you in my life forever,
And you need me in yours too,
Even if all we'll ever be
Is the best of friends till the end.

    And though it saddens me
    That all we'll ever really be is friends
    As that's how fate
    Has dealt its cards,

I will always hope for more,
And this will keep me going,
Keep me hanging on to something
Really special, magical, comforting.

    I will dream of walking
    With you hand in hand,
    Cuddling beside you under the stars,
    Kissing your tender lips,

Melting into you
As you melt into me
Without ever parting,
Just staying in this moment forever.

A Crimson Tide | Poetry by Lena Kovadlo

~ YOUR LETTERS FROM THE SEA ~
August 27, 2009

An ink stained paper
    With words lost in time
        Flew onto the window
            Of my darkening life.

The words were your story
    Of your journey through time,
        Of your days on that vessel
            Slipping by from my life.

A skiff on a giant,
    You waved your good-bye,
        Got lost in the ocean,
            Hid away from my eye.

And the memory of you
    In the waters of ink
        Are the stains I swim through,
            To feel you, to think.

~ ALONE TRYING TO FIND ~
March 29, 2009

Alone here
Trying to find
        The truth
        Within the lies,
                The lies
                Within the truth.

Alone here
Trying to find
        The truth,
        The lies

                Of being here,
                Of being alone,
                      Of living
                      Without you.

~ CAN'T STAND THESE TWO ~
March 29, 2009

Their sweet play makes me sick.
Their presence makes me vomit.
I can't stand the sight of these two
'Cause I don't have what they have
And I never will.

~ EVERYWHERE ~
March 5, 2009

The faces I see in the crowd
Remind me of you.

You are in everything I see,
Everywhere I go,
Whatever I do.

You live inside me,
And are there with me
Every waking moment of every day.

That's the way it will be
Until we both take the journey to eternity.

~ ONE ENTITY ~
March 3, 2009

You and I are one entity
We complete each other in every way
Together we are unstoppable
Our love is unbreakable
We are two halves of a whole

With you everything is perfect
Like a fairy tale world I am in
I hope it remains that way forever
Because then my world
Will never experience a rainy day
Filled with endless bitter taste

~ DAYDREAMING PRINCESS ~
March 3, 2009

The princess rests in her armchair
Daydreaming about her prince.
They are strolling through the park
Along with the chirping birds,
The caressing wind,
The warming sun up above.

A smile lights up her face
As she starts to sing a tune,
Sweet, melodic, full of passion;
A song about her prince,
A very special person
Whom the princess can't live without.

~ SOMETHING THAT WILL NEVER BE ~
February 26, 2009

I wanted you in my life forever.
I did not care about titles,
About what we were to each other.
All I wanted was for you to be here,
You and I hanging out
Chatting away about anything
Or nothing at all.
I just wanted to be in your presence,
Wanted to know I am cared about.
But all that never happened,
And I was left with nothing but a want,
A desire that would never be real.

~ POLINA BRANDIS ACROSTIC ~
February 25, 2009

Poised ballerina
On the carousel of love
Lifting the veil
Inside wounded hearts
Never falling
Always soaring

Branding us with smiles
Rotating and affectionate
And glistening our tears
Nurtured by sweet juices
Doses of overflowing happiness
Inside our souls
Sprinkled on our hearts

~ UNWANTED REALITY ~
February 12, 2009

Her lips are moving.
Unaware of what escapes from within,
The guy next to her smiles,
Gives out a chuckle,
Drinks up all the playful banter
That seems to mirror his feelings.

In the end things crack,
And his mind settles on the unwanted reality.
He was cast as the leading star,
A puppet on a string,
Caught in the play
He didn't know he was a part of.

The show is over,
The curtains drawn,
Leaving him in the company of the bottle,
The curling smoke of the cigar,
The deafening silence of his thoughts, and surroundings;
Something that will never be again.

~ FRIENDSHIP ~
February 8, 2009

With a glistening tear I cherish your friendship;
A rare gem to be treasured for life.
With a heartwarming smile I'll forever adore you.
You're my Fin, my best friend
Through the day, through the night.

~ HIDDEN INSIDE MY TREASURE ~
January 5, 2009

I pass on my treasure
From me to you
And wish you the best
In all that you do

I hope that your days
Are filled with love
With laughter and happiness
Hanging above

Dive into this book
And maybe you'll find
The pieces of you
Hidden inside

~ MY SOUL EXPOSED ~
December 7, 2008

I poured out my soul to you from a glass
And I drained myself from the secrets no less
You drank them all up and went your own way
And now I'm unsure if the secrets will stay
Will you bury them deep in your mind and forget
Or will you pass them on to the others and let
Let my soul be exposed to the folk of the world
And tell them my story that should never be told

A Crimson Tide | Poetry by Lena Kovadlo

~ VANISHED ~
October 2, 2008

I've heard your apologies many times
Heard you say that you're sorry
Sorry for letting weeks go by
Without writing me
Heard you reassure me
That we are still friends
That you really care about me
And that you will never vanish from my life

Yes I believed every word you said
Believed that we are really friends
But I stopped feeling that way
Because you are not around
And you do not write me
I feel alone and abandoned
And I feel like you vanished from my life
Never to return

Whether it was your choice
Or just how life goes
You are not here with me
And your existence cannot be traced
Because you vanished
Never to return

A Crimson Tide | Poetry by Lena Kovadlo

~ WHERE WOULD I BE WITHOUT YOU? ~
August 11, 2008

Where would I be without you
But alone in this crazy world
A world where no one understands me
Or tries to look within my soul
But only see, what they choose to see
And see what they think should be
Yet not who I really am inside and out

Without you I'd be lost forever
Lost inside myself, inside this hell
But with you I am free
And my world is full of meaning
And my life no longer a hole
Through which I stumble and fall
Because I am here with you

A Crimson Tide | Poetry by Lena Kovadlo

~ DROWN IN DREAMS OF YOU ~
June 1, 2008

It's time to bare myself for night
And drown in dreams of you so right
And fly away where you and me
Are in Atlantis, two souls so free

~ CLOSE IN OUR DREAM ~
June 1, 2008

You will have fun once you're in bed
You'll feel me close beside you and
You'll dream of me under the stars
And drown in the mystery of ours

~ RIGHT HERE FOR YOU ~
May 26, 2008

Don't be upset
I'll be right here
I'm gonna make sure
You don't shed a tear
And if you do
I'll wipe it away
'Cause I want you to have
The brightest of days

~ WITH YOU ON MY MIND ~
May 26, 2008

I'll be thinking of you
All through the night
I'll be thinking of you
All through the day
And I know that everything
Will be okay
With you I will soar
Straight into the skies
And tears of sorrow
Will not leave my eyes

A Crimson Tide | Poetry by Lena Kovadlo

~ MISS YOU MY CURE ~
May 26, 2008

I miss you more than words can say
I miss you each and every day
You're on my mind and in my heart
From you I never want to part
For you're the cure for aches and pains
That ever try to come my way
And you're the guiding light I see
With you I feel alive and free

~ ALL THAT YOU DREAM ~
May 22, 2008

Have the sweetest of dreams
And the brightest of smiles
As you sail away
To the stars in the night

And may all that you dream
Only fill you with love
And the magic and beauty
That burns deep in your heart

And may that never change
May you never taste sorrow
For a soul as sweet as you
Deserves the brightest tomorrows

~ I'LL BE WITH YOU ~
December 10, 2007

I'll be with you with when you're in pain
To make sure you don't hurt again
I'll be with you when tears fall
I'll be right there when you call
I'll never let you drown in sorrow
With me you'll always see a brighter tomorrow

~ BLOCKED ~
November 24, 2007

My feelings for you are so strong
So why can't I write you this song
I sit here alone in the dark
The words lack the beauty and spark
What comes into life only dies
And inside my whole being it cries
For this promised gift cannot be born
Though the passion burns strong in my soul
I am blocked and my battle seems lost
Just when I need my talent the most
And that troubles and tortures me so
That the words from my heart cannot grow
That my promise is yet to be true
That my gift can't be given to you
And these tears they stain my face
For this trouble I cannot erase
So until all is perfect and done
Seems I'll find it hard to go on
'Cause I'll always be haunted and blue
Till this song will be written for you
And though love you'll say it's okay
I won't rest till the words find their way
Through the endless sweating and tears
Into a masterpiece you'll cherish for years

A Crimson Tide | Poetry by Lena Kovadlo

~ AUTOGRAPH POEM ~
October 25, 2007

Now that my treasure is yours to keep
My heart once empty became complete
And I find myself swimming in nothing but bliss
Hoping to find my days just like this
Trapped in this heavenly moment so dear
With you on my mind, in my heart, and so near

~ YOU ARE THE SONG, YOU ARE THE FIRE ~
August 7, 2007

You are the song inside my heart
That echoes through the day
That touches me so deeply
More than mere words can say

You are the fire within my soul
That flames inside so bright
And one that won't extinguish
And will guide me through the night

~ TO DREAM OF YOU ~
August 7, 2007

To dream of you is pure pleasure
That brings you closer to my heart
And every scene I'll always treasure
For from my heart you'll never part

You'll linger there with days' passing
Warming my spirit and my soul
And my whole being you'll be caressing
There with your presence taking hold

~ YOU ARE ~
August 4, 2007

You're my bedtime story
You're my shooting star
You're my guiding light
To magic dreams afar

You're my happy ending
Every craving too
A book I can't put down
No matter what I do

~ MOUTHWATERING DELIGHT ~
August 2, 2007

My mouthwatering delight
Oh how you sweeten up the night
Juices flow from you to me
I drown there in ecstasy
You I devour luscious treat
Surrender in sleepless defeat

~ MY WORDS ~
August 1, 2007

Now don't you fear I'll keep you fed
My words they'll never become dead
They will imprint there in your head
They'll melt your heart and leave you glad

~ MELODIC EMBRACE ~
August 1, 2007

Our bodies locked in tight embrace
Electric jolts begin to race
And our hearts quake in rhythmic beat
Singing a melody so sweet

~ HEAVENLY LOVE ~
July 11, 2007

We touched the sun
And found peace
Beyond the clouds
Of heavenly love

A Crimson Tide | Poetry by Lena Kovadlo

~ DON'T GIVE UP ~
January 21, 2007

Find a way to control the motion
Of the heart's complex emotion
And don't give up on love and lust
For without them you'll find life just
A lonely journey through the years
A wounded heart that never heals
Just give it time and you'll soar above
The magic and beauty of mysterious love

~ WAITING ~
January 18, 2007

I wait and wait for your response
But all I see is page of white
No words from you
What can I do
To stop this yearning
Hear from you
To let me know
Just how you feel
About what my heart revealed
Have you been affected
Why have you vanished
Can't stand it, it's killing me
These tears of pain

THE BLACK VEIL

Our journey through life is such that we must leave it behind at some point. Sometimes we move on at a very young age. Sometimes we are blessed with the gift of being able to savor all that life has to offer for many, many years and when we finally pass we are well into our years.

Though death and the loss of loved ones is very much a part of life it is not something that we look forward to; it is not something that we constantly think about. If anything, we want to stay away from this topic because it is heartbreaking, and painful. It is difficult to cope with and can scar us for life.

Poetry in this section will focus on death – the passing of loved ones and dear ones, coping with the loss, witnessing with our very own eyes as they slip away from us, and anything else related to this devastating and sorrowful part of our existence.

A Crimson Tide | Poetry by Lena Kovadlo

~ LAID TO REST ~
June 15, 2012

Everyone stood in hushed silence
As the four men in navy colored uniforms
Dug out the dirt from the ground
And lowered the large brown casket
Down into the cold hollow ground

It was a warm sunny day outside
But the birds weren't chirping
Their beautiful melodies
Instead the roar of the planes
Filled the clear blue sky
Breaking the deafening silence

One by one the men, women, and children
All dressed in black
Threw the dirt onto the casket
Covering it until it was hidden from view
It was the final good-bye and parting
From the one they held dear in their hearts

No longer would he be in their lives physically
But he would always be present spiritually
In photographs, in the air above
And more importantly in their hearts and souls
As the memory of him
And the love for him
They held dear
Would always live on and on

~ HE LAY THERE ON DISPLAY ~
June 15, 2012

He lay there in his deep brown bed
Lifeless, peacefully dreaming
In a room full of people who sobbed
Talked of his passing
And remembered all the wonderful moments
They've shared together all these years

A stranger he lay there on display
His face and expression unrecognizable
To those who knew him so well

No longer was there a spark in his eyes
Or a light illuminating from within him
He was hollow and hard as stone
Both inside and out

His time came upon him unexpectedly
And changed him into the man
No one thought he'd become

He seemed a stranger
But they all knew his soul would rise once more
And shine upon the world
Once they laid him to rest

~ HIS OTHER HALF ~
June 18, 2012

She was his whole world
The center of his universe
A part of him he couldn't live without
Then one night as they talked
Her voice became hushed
And she drifted off for the night
He didn't want to disturb her so let her be
When he woke up the next morning
She lay in a position he'd never seen her in
Her body frozen, her eyes closed tight
He whispered to her
But she didn't respond
He knew then that she had left him
And a part of him vanished along with her
People told him to go out
To find his other half
But he wouldn't do such a thing
The only person who would ever be
His other half was his wife
But she was no longer with him

~ IT'S TIME FOR YOU TO LEARN HOW TO DRIVE ~
June 13, 2012

It's time for you to learn how to drive
He whispered to her Sunday morning
While they lounged on their cozy bed.

But honey, you know how I get
When it comes to driving –
Sweaty, shaking hands,
Crippling fear.
I can't get behind the wheel.

I know you've been very tired lately.
I promise I won't ask you
To drive me anywhere for a while.
Now go get some rest.
We have a while yet before it's time to wake up.
She whispered back to him.

Thank you. I could use a little more sleep
He said, slowly closing his eyes.

Half an hour passed.
She looked at her husband
Lying peacefully under the blanket.
She lay there looking at him, smiling,
Warmed by the closeness of him,
On the bed they had shared for over 35 years.

A Crimson Tide | Poetry by Lena Kovadlo

She drifted off for a while.
But then was woken up by a startling scream.
HELP! SOMEBODY HELP ME!

She quickly opened her eyes
To see what was going on.
Turning to look at her husband
She could see him lying on his stomach,
Head turned to the wall,
His left hand hanging off the bed.

She shook her husband,
Telling him to wake up,
Asking him what was the matter,
But there was no response.

She got up off the bed
And went to stand at his bedside.
His eyes were closed.
His breath on mute.

She touched his hand,
Felt for his pulse,
But felt nothing.

She started to sob.
And through the tears she heard him whisper
It's time for you learn how to drive.

Why after all these years did he tell her this?
Perhaps deep inside
He felt that his end was coming.

A Crimson Tide | Poetry by Lena Kovadlo

~ THE POND ~
May 7, 2012

She waited for him by the swings
Near the pond where they first met
That sunny glorious day.
She swung herself higher and higher,
Reaching for the clouds, for the memories
They shared on that day and beyond.

Half an hour passed in a blur
And dizziness overcame her, so strong.
She thought she saw him on the swing
Flying next to her in a similar rhythm.
She reached out her right hand to the swing
But there was no one there but wind
Making the swing soar up to the heavens.

A tear fell down her face
At his absence she couldn't bare,
At their one year anniversary
That she would be spending alone.

Through the heavy downpour
She thought she saw him again
Standing by the pond's willow tree
Feeding a family of ducks.
He glanced at her for a brief moment –
A smile so radiant, so captivating.

A Crimson Tide | Poetry by Lena Kovadlo

Then he knelt down on one knee
And removed a black velvet box
From inside his navy jacket.
He opened the box
And a ring shone in the sunlight –
A white gold band with a precious pearl
Surrounded by brilliant diamonds.

I love you Jane. Will you marry me?
He whispered in the breeze.
I love you Ben. Of course I will marry you.
She whispered back to him.

She jumped off the swings and ran to him,
Ran to the pond with open arms,
But she didn't stop running.
She ran and ran until she fell into the pond
Knowing that he wasn't there on bended knee
And the pearl ring was on display in the store.

The pond had taken him away from her,
And it was the only portal
That would unite them once more
On this sunny glorious day.

A Crimson Tide | Poetry by Lena Kovadlo

~ HEART FILLED WITH ARIAS ~
April 13, 2012

He opens the petite closet
For the first time in months
And stares at the unworn clothes,
Inhaling the familiar scent of her perfume
That still lingers in the air.

He removes the silk blouse,
Waiting crisp and ironed,
Ready to be worn to daycare,
And clings it to his chest
As if she is there in the room.

With familiar tears escaping from within,
He places the blouse back on the rack,
And makes his way to the living room,
Where she awaits his beautiful solos,
With a red rose in her hands.

He looks deep into her sparkling eyes
And serenades her with his collection of arias
That she's come to appreciate over the years.
His voice doesn't waver as the notes,
Full of delicate passion, fill the empty room.

As the final notes of the concluding aria
Escape from within him, hours later,
He removes her portrait from the wall,
Clutches it to his beating heart,
And tenderly brushes his lips against hers.

A Crimson Tide | Poetry by Lena Kovadlo

Jane, I love you sweetheart.
I hope you enjoyed those arias.
He whispers, hanging the portrait
On its familiar hiding place
Between the open windows.

Tomorrow will be another day filled with song,
Another day with his beloved wife
That he will treasure forever in his heart,
For it will always be filled with the familiar arias
She has come to appreciate through the years.

~ MY FINAL GOOD-BYE ~
May 7, 2012

I knew one day your time would come
For you to move on to the heavens
I never imagined it would come so soon
Never pictured myself seeing your limp
Lifeless body covered in purple
Your arms hanging off your once cozy bed
Never thought this is how I'd be saying
My final good-bye to you
That this is how we would forever part

A Crimson Tide | Poetry by Lena Kovadlo

~ NOWHERE TO BE FOUND ~
February 2, 2012

I come to visit you
amongst the tombstones
and piles of dirt; to place
some carnations and stones
onto your new underground
lair; to reminisce about the
days that passed and talk
of days to come.

I come to say hello,
come to say how much
I miss you, how much I love
you. My eyes scan for
your name tag but it is
nowhere to be found.

I wonder if you've been
evicted from your new home,
or if I've simply come to the
wrong address. Perhaps you're
still there in your old home
lying next to your husband
peacefully dreaming.

A Crimson Tide | Poetry by Lena Kovadlo

~ YOUR PRESENCE TAKING ME APART ~
February 2, 2012

You've moved on to a better place
Yet you still linger here
For you are always on my mind

> Your face clear as the baby blue sky
> Looks up into mine
> So sweet, gentle, and carefree

I talk to you
As if you were here in person
I tell you my side of the story
And wait for you to tell me yours

> Your eyes are hollow yet burn like the sun
> Looking through my soul
> Deep into all the pieces of me
> Taking me apart bit by bit

Letting me know I'm slowly falling apart
Slowly fading from who I can become
From who I'm meant to be

> Letting me know that it is only I
> Who can put me back together again
> It is only I who can write the story of my life
> The story that is meant to unfold

~ ETERNAL SLUMBER ~
August 31, 2011

I entered your room
To find you so still and quiet
Lying in your queen-sized bed
Peacefully sleeping

I didn't want to disturb you
But it didn't matter anyway
Because you were in eternal slumber
That took you away to a better place

~ LEFT US ~
August 31, 2011

So soon you left us
To wander this earth alone
Without a sign you were planning to leave
The unshed tears kept pouring out
And they will forever fall
Because you will never return to us
Until we meet in another life

~ MEMORIES ~
September 6, 2010

A stone engraved in memories
Of a life long passed
But never-to-be forgotten,
By those who lived beside it,
Those who cherished it,
Stands tall among the rising grass.
The scattered petals of daisies
A reminder of *I do*'s and *I do not*'s,
Of a love slipping by but always returning,
As new petals grow once more
Into the awakening of a new life,
A new love that will always be carved in stone.

~ NO LONGER HERE ~
December 3, 2010

He took the journey
To a better place
No more suffering
No more darkened days
May he rest in peace
May he soar above
Always, he'll be missed
And forever loved

~ YOUR BROTHER ~
February 1, 2010

Your brother will always live around you,
Live inside you and surround you.
Your brother will be your angel for life
To watch over you and make sure you're all right.

~ DAY OF REMEMBRANCE ~
November 30, 2009

Here I am staring out the window...
The rain is beating down like a faucet
In sync with the tears that shower my face.
I am lost in the river of emotions,
Washing over me on this day of remembrance.

I float back to the days of you and I,
To a time when we swam together,
To a time when our waves of connection,
Our waves of attraction and love, never died,
When the promises of our flow through time
Were sweet, filled with streams of hope and love,
When I felt better days on the horizon,
When my dreams of eternal happiness with you seemed real.

Now, when the waves came crashing down
On you and I, and what could have been,
When my dreams are only dreams that would never be real,
I sit here on this day of remembrance,
Drowning in my own tears,
Drowning in the memories that will never be again.

A Crimson Tide | Poetry by Lena Kovadlo

DARKENING THE PALE

At times we go through these dark moments in our life that not only tend to be intense, but also can make us keep to ourselves. We wish for things to be different. We battle with ourselves, our existence and our surroundings, trying to rationalize what is happening around us, what we are meant to be doing, who we are meant to be. It is a time of reflection, a time when we dig deep into ourselves and try to make sense of all that is happening.

All the poetry found in this section will in some way be related to what I've mentioned above. Topics will include eating disorders, self-image issues, inner battles, personal struggles, fear, other psychological issues, things of a philosophical nature, things that are dark, things that are metaphorical and more...

~ EMBRACED BY THE DARKNESS ~
October 24, 2012

Rotten is the day
The dark clouds covering
Everything in their wake
Including my heart
That has seen the decay of love
That has inhaled the stench of death
That has felt the sharp slicing of skin
Of words filled with life's last breath
As the remains of the sun's rays
Hide behind the silent night
Leaving me alone
To be embraced by the darkness
That will remain
Until you and I reunite
And the sun will wake once more
From its eternal slumber

~ CAN'T GO BACK TO THE PAST ~
July 7, 2012

You can't reverse time
Can't take back hurtful things you said
Can't take back the things you've done
Can't take back all you regret

You can't go back to the past
Can't undo anything, can't alter it
But you can take the past
And turn it into the future
Changing the outcome
To what you've always
Wanted it to be

~ BITTERNESS ~
May 30, 2012

There's a bitterness in my heart
That spreads through me like lava
Into every piece of me
Into my very existence

Every day I harden more and more
As it destroys all my hopes and dreams
Into nothing but bitter ash

No longer can I go on
Without feeling the hot sting
Seep through me
Sinking deep to the core of me

I am destroyed
Becoming hard as stone
Forever tormented
By the things that have vanished
By things that won't be reborn
Because of the bitterness
That has taken over my ashen heart

~ THE MIRROR ~
April 26, 2012

The mirror distorts her beauty
Making her a stranger in her own body
Her face is lost, her eyes hollow
Her smile fading with the sun
Nothing about her speaks "that's me"
But that's only what the mirror says
And what she chooses to believe
To everyone else she is the same as ever
Still the beautiful girl they've come to know
Over the years

~ THE LAST TO KNOW ~
April 17, 2012

Why am I always the last to know
About things I should be aware of

      Why does the news travel anywhere
      But in my direction

           Why do I find myself behind the pack
           Invisible, unimportant, forgotten

                Why am I always the last to know

~ WAITING TO BE RELEASED ~
March 12, 2012

No money in the world
Is worth the emotional torture
Of being here day by day
Waiting for the day to end
Waiting to be released
From the four walls that trap me here
With no way of escaping into my freedom

~ I'M A STRANGER ~
March 9, 2012

Here I am and I'm still breathing
But the breath is not my own
Someone else lives deep inside me
Someone I have never known

I'm a stranger in my body
I'm a stranger in my head
Where the real me is hiding
Is a mystery that has led

Me to question my existence
Who I am and meant to be
I am trapped inside the body
That has yet to set me free

A Crimson Tide | Poetry by Lena Kovadlo

~ FROZEN HEART ~
March 9, 2012

Crystal droplets glisten across my face
As I gaze out into the misty air
The sun slowly peeking through the gray skies

The air thickens around me
And I can no longer feel my breath
The rise and fall of my chest

All I feel are the crystal droplets
Leaving icy marks across my face
Forever imprinted there for all to see

I do not wish to hide the scars etched in my soul
I do not wish to conceal the memories
That will forever glow inside my frozen heart

I do not wish to be thawed of emotion
For it is what makes me who I am
A soul who bares it all to the world

~ TRAPPED IN THE CELL ~
March 8, 2012

I am trapped in the cell
    Its bars blocking the air
Suffocating me
    As I wait for the crawling day to end
For the bars to release me once more
    Into the yearning freedom
That I crave to breathe
    While I am trapped in the cell
I wish to escape from
    Why do I find myself
Trapped in this cell
    When I didn't want to be
There in the first place

~ IT ALL SEEMS LIKE A DREAM ~
February 12, 2012

I roam the streets I've come to know

Visit familiar places

      Perform the tasks I'm used to

           Yet it all seems like a dream

    Like I am watching someone else

Going through what I'm going through

And I'm just stuck in a place I can't escape

~ A SCARED CHILD LIVES WITHIN ~
February 12, 2012

Inside her lives a scared child
Afraid of taking charge
Afraid of defending who she is
And wants to be in this world
Afraid of committing to the love
That comes her way
Afraid of the things that matter
She doesn't live life
She merely exists
Awaiting her time to leave it all behind

~ DREAM I YEARN FOR IN MY MIND ~
February 2, 2012

I yearn for change to come
And transport me into a world
I dream of in my mind
A world where everything
Falls into its rightful place
And all the worries
Are nowhere to be found

~ FEAR ~
February 2, 2012

For everything that can happen
Everything that can become real
All is buried underground
Resting until courage rises above and conquers

A Crimson Tide | Poetry by Lena Kovadlo

~ TRYING TO MAKE THE FERRY ~
November 7, 2011

Running
        Breathless
                Panting
Heels thumping against the ground
Heavy bags hitting against their legs
They run as if life depends on it
Only to have the door
        Slammed in their face
They won't get home on time
But at least they got their exercise

A Crimson Tide | Poetry by Lena Kovadlo

~ WHAT THE MIRROR ALWAYS SAYS ~
November 8, 2011

Alone with a giant mirror,
Staring at her reflection,
She sees the truth others deny...

Her belly protrudes from her t-shirt
Like a ripened watermelon.
Her legs are heavy,
Making her skinny jeans rip at the seams.
Fat is hanging every which way,
From her legs, her arms, her face, her stomach,
From every inch of her undesired silhouette.

Nothing fits her deformed body.
Nothing feels right against her skin.
She wants to tear off her clothes
But it will only reveal what she yearns to hide.

She stands there frozen,
Staring at her reflection,
A loud voice escaping from the mirror,
"You're a FAT, ugly freak!
No food must enter your body!
I will not let you live until you've lost it all!"

Tears spill from her face,
And she fills with rage,
Vowing never to let food in.

A Crimson Tide | Poetry by Lena Kovadlo

Every time she looks at her reflection in the mirror,
All she hears is "you're a FAT, ugly freak!"
Even when her clothes sag like a rag,
And her jeans fall to the floor,
Even when there is nothing left of her but bones,
Even when she's lost it all,
She is still a FAT, ugly freak, and always will be.
That's what the mirror always says.

~ I AM A FLOWER ~
April 30, 2011

I am a flower on display
My petals picked one by one
Trying to reveal the real me
But who am I really

To you I am a flower
To you I am beautiful
Every piece of me
Both inside and out

~ THE TREE ~
April 30, 2011

I am
no longer
the tree I used
to be – blooming,
expanding, penetrated
with life. Now I am naked,
my branches sagging, the bark
peeling off, the earth withering
beneath me. You are the only one
who can breathe
life into me; to
make me whole
again; to turn
me into the tree
I used to be.

~ SAFE ~
April 30, 2011

She locks herself up in her room
With no desire to face life's struggles

>It is there that she is safe
>Safe from the world she yearns to leave behind
>
>It is there that she finds escape
>Finds herself weightlessly floating

It is there that her life is carefree
Free of the obstacles that destroy her

~ COUCH POTATO ~
April 2, 2010

The couch is your grave
You are trapped there with no escape
No sign of life
No desire for action
Leaving you on that couch
In deep eternal slumber
As days pass you by

~ INVISIBLE PUPPY ~
April 2, 2010

She lies on the staircase,
Her head hanging down,
Sorrow seeping through every core.
Her long, untamed hair
Hiding her beauty,
Blinding her eyes,
Making her invisible to the world.

    She lies on the staircase
    Long forgotten,
    Waiting for a sign of life,
    For a drop of water,
    For a crumb of food,
    But it looks like it will never come,
    Leaving her invisible on that staircase,
    Making her even more unrecognizable to the world.

~ TAKEN AWAY ~
January 19, 2010

The raging seas took her away
From the comfort
Of the familiar waters
She grew safe around.

    She was now caught in the roaring tide;
    Sinking deep into the torrent of emotions,
    That seemed to drown her
    With every break.

        Would she ever swim back to shore,
        Back to the familiar waters,
        Back to the comfort
        That surrounded her with every wake?

            Only time's flow would tell ...

~ A DREAM OR NOT? ~
January 12, 2010

I dreamed a dream
        In which I flew
               From skies above,
                      From skies of blue.

                And then these skies,
          They turned to black.
      With eyes of red,
The bats attacked.

They flew and flew
        Straight through my heart,
                With streaks of red
                      That left their mark.

                I flew and flew
          To lands below,
      With streaks of red
That overflowed.

A Crimson Tide | Poetry by Lena Kovadlo

Then I awoke,
    And through the mirror,
        Saw my reflection
            Getting clearer.

        My eyes were red,
      My body black,
    My heart a hole,
And I wreck.

The dream I dreamed
    Wasn't just a dream;
        I was attacked
           By bats it seemed.

        And those bats
      Were love gone by
    That left me here
Drained here to die...

~ IN THIS PLACE ~
November 17, 2009 & November 23, 2009

In this place I roam alone
A place I cannot call my own
I want to leave it all behind
I gotta go, I gotta find
My peace at last
Eternal peace
Cannot exist here like this
'Cause every day I'm falling down
Can't get back up
Can't get around
Don't know where I'm going
Or where I'll end up
But one thing is for certain
I know I've had enough

~ UNCONTROLLABLE FEAR ~
October 6, 2009

Deep inside her reigns a fear she can't control
She doesn't know what that fear is
But she knows it controls her life
Deep to the point where she is afraid
To take that first step
To make that first move
She doesn't know how to conquer this fear
And lets it envelop her
In turn leaving her in a place
She does not desire to be

~ WANDERING WOUNDS ~
May 18, 2009

Wandering wounds
For the wounded
For healing
For finding yourself
For believing
For dealing
With things that surround us
Embrace us
Affect us
These wandering wounds
They will never reject us
There's no life without them
In time they will heal
And always remind us
Our existence is real
So those that are wounded
Those yet to be too
Let these wandering wounds
Be a life guide for you

~ THE WORDS ~
March 30, 2009

I'm lost deep in the words
        That fill the empty pages.
They penetrate every crevice
        Of my mind,
Of my flesh.

Everything around me isn't there.
        It's just me and the words on the page.
I hear nothing but silence.
        It speaks to me louder than noise,
Louder than words you speak.

I swim in these words.
        I live in these words.
I am now the words on the pages
        That once seemed empty
When in reality they were
        Never empty to begin with.

You were just blind
        To what was really there
All along.

~ MISSING PIECES ~
March 29, 2009

    Missing   pieces
           Never
  To be   found
        Again,
  Never   to be
        Put
  Together   in full,
       Back
 To what   once was
     The past,
The present,   the future.

~ ALIVE BUT DEAD ~
March 6, 2009

Your flesh is alive,
Yet you are dead.
Your face shows no emotion.
Your eyes are hollow.
There is no bounce in your step,
No melody in your voice,
No sun in your smile.
Your arms are sagging twigs,
Your body curled into a question mark.
You roam each passing day physically alive,
Yet psychologically and spiritually you are dead.
There is no point in living
When each passing day means nothing
And there is nothing to look forward to at all.

~ NORMAL OR NOT ~
March 5, 2009

I've got sunny days.
I've got rainy days.
    They come and go
    Like a roller coaster
Up and down,
Left and right.

I ride these emotional cycles every day
And wonder what it all means.
    Different emotions make things more exciting
    But a repeating pattern day in and day out
It isn't normal to experience.
Or is it normal after all?

I mean what is normal really?
Are any of us really normal?
    Is what we experience anything normal?
    How do we know what normal really is?

Maybe what we deem normal is really abnormal,
And what's abnormal is really normal.
    What's normal? What's not?
    How do we really know?

~ NEVER-ENDING TAPE ~
February 26, 2009

She hides under the table,
Curled into a ball with her teddy.
Echoes of anger and broken china
Resonate all around.

>She is frozen in terror
>By the movie playing above.
>She wills to be deaf and blind
>To the action in the room.

It's all a never-ending tape
Stuck in a broken VCR
That cannot be PAUSED,
STOPPED, or EJECTED.

>Unable to turn off her senses,
>Or mute the scene of her parents,
>She remains in the safety of the table
>And waits for the tape to die.

~ IMMUNE ~
February 25, 2009

You tell me how to think,
Tell me how to act,
Tell me how to dress;
You program me with your mind,
With your eyes,
With your voice.

You debug me inch by inch
Thinking I won't crash,
But your test fails.
There is a bug inside me.
You can try to crack the code
But it cannot be fixed.

The bug is my willpower,
My inner strength
That fights against your brainwash,
And fully repels
Your preconceived image
Of the person I should be.

The vision you have is yours alone;
It is not mine nor will ever be.
I have eyes of my own,
Deep eyes that see through your plan
To turn me into something I am not
Nor ever intend to be.

A Crimson Tide | Poetry by Lena Kovadlo

You can program me to your liking,
But you're better off directing your energy
Towards someone else,
Someone who is not immune to your virus,
A robot that will follow every command
You code into his brain.

I cannot be automated,
I cannot be altered
Or rewired by anyone.
The only one who can transform me is me;

I have programmed my mind
To crash your code,
To reroute your flow chart
Elsewhere but in my direction.
So go into shut down mode
And find another pc to infect.

~ LONELY PAPER ~
January 30, 2009

The lonely paper floats in the breeze,
    Aged with forgotten memories.
        An ink coated feather rests atop,
            Waiting with the passing of time
For a hand to leave its mark
            On the world, on its children,
    Both the living and the dead,
    The visible and the not,
On everything that lies in its wake.

~ LOST ~
January 30, 2009

Your lips move in excited chatter.
I sit there, eyes fixed on their movement,
Yet I am deaf to the sound that escapes from within,
Blind to the movement of the flesh,
Unaware of your presence beside me.

I am lost in my own thoughts
Sinking deeper and deeper
Into every dissected spec of my lingering mind.

My flesh is here, yet I am in another world,
Somewhere passed oceans and mountains high
Where no one can reach me,
Where no one knows of my existence,
Where I am a secret,
A treasure waiting to be found.

A Crimson Tide | Poetry by Lena Kovadlo

~ THIS DIMENSION ~
January 28, 2009

I see an ocean of faces surround me.
Hear the murmur of the packaged crowd.
Feel the caress of the wind on my skin.
Feel the blinding light shine in my eyes.

I am not alone at this given moment,
But everything is but a blur around me.
I am trapped inside this dimension;
It's just me and the deafening silence.

I stand here frozen in time,
My body moving like a Ferris wheel,
Surrounded by a cloud of ghostly rays
And droplets of dew that glisten my face.

There is a presence of something familiar,
Yet I cannot touch it, or see it;
I can only feel it surround me in a tight hold,
Gripping me like a chained prisoner.

A Crimson Tide | Poetry by Lena Kovadlo

Is that me standing in the mist of gray,
Or am I being possessed by another being,
Taking control over all that I am,
All that I thought I was?

What is the purpose of my existence?
How is my life meant to unfold?
What am I meant to accomplish
In this ever changing realm of the unknown?

These are the puzzling questions,
To which the answers remain a mystery.
A secret locked with the passing of time,
Whose meaning my mind has yet to dissect.

~ NOTHING MATTERS ~
January 26, 2009

I see a glimpse of you,
Wherever I go,
Wherever I turn,
And I wonder are you really here,
Or just a hologram I conjured up in my mind
To make it seem that you care
About me, about us,
About what we can become,
About what we've been through.

I wonder why it seems you're always here,
Yet I can never reach you or catch you.
I wonder how you go on
As if we've never met,
As if I don't exist,
As if nothing matters,
Not I, nor you, nor us,
Not what was or could ever be.

Nothing really matters when it should
Because what matters is not nothing.
It is something with a purpose,
Something deep no matter how simple;
Everything has depth,
Even nothing has depth.

A Crimson Tide | Poetry by Lena Kovadlo

Depth is not nothing;
It is something that nothing holds,
Something that's there for us to grasp.
But do we want to grasp it?
Do we want to acknowledge it?
This nothing that is something,
This depth that lives inside us,
In mind, body, and spirit,
This depth that can never be left behind.

A Crimson Tide | Poetry by Lena Kovadlo

~ DECISIONS ~
October 17, 2008

My head is a jungle of thoughts
Overflowing
      Overlapping
Conflicting
With decisions hanging over me

I separate the pros and the cons
Try to ponder the best action
The best route to take
But can't set both feet on either side

I find myself trapped in confusion
Trapped in uncertainty
Trapped in fear
And I have no clue
How to get out of it

Because a decision must be made
One that can alter my life
In a good way
And in a bad way
A decision that must be made on the fly
And one where the outcome is unclear

~ MIDNIGHT SCREAMS ~
October 6, 2008

She lays in bed there in the dark.
The door is locked, the windows shut.
The only light is of the moon,
And of the stars that hang above.

> There's not a soul in the home,
> It's only her and teddy there.
> Who knows what lurks down below,
> Three stories down in the lair.

The silence, deafening, surrounds
As Lilly hides under the covers.
Her sleep has faded as she listens
To midnight screams that drag the hours.

> With teddy wrapped around her tight,
> She tries to talk herself to sleep,
> Yet feels no comfort in the room.
> Her thoughts, disturbing, start to creep.

She shakes with shivers on her flesh,
And prays for night to hide away.
She dreads the dark and yearns for light,
To rescue her from ghostly rays.

> At last her eyes with blind vision,
> They drift her to the land of dreams.
> And she no longer weeps in silence,
> Attuned to endless midnight screams.

~ HAUNTING ME ~
October 2, 2008

There you are creeping into my mind
Making a home for yourself in every corner
Never intending to leave and let me be
Never wanting anything else
But to haunt me at every turn
To haunt my every thought
To haunt my every move

I wish you would just let me be
Let me live my life without your presence
I have been tortured enough
I have been haunted too much
And I don't want any more suffering
I just want to be at ease and at peace
And with you around that is never going to be

A Crimson Tide | Poetry by Lena Kovadlo

~ A CHEATER'S HEART ~
June 30, 2008

My soul bleeds from a cheater's heart
The heart that belongs to me
The heart that weeps with tears
I am cheating myself in this game of life
This game which I cannot win

I battle every waking moment of every day
To be a free soul
To release myself from this mess
From everything that needs to change
To do what I crave for
To do what I need to do
To finally make things right
To live life the way I want to live it
Yet I do not do those things
Because my heart won't let me

It is a scared child consumed by fear
Fear of what's to come
Fear of coming short
Fear of failing
And so here I am
Living every waking moment of every day
Bleeding from a cheater's heart

The heart that belongs to me
The heart that weeps with tears
Living a life without change
A life that will never make me a free soul
A life that will only cause me to bleed
Every waking moment of every day

~ TRAPPED WITHIN I SURRENDER ~
June 19, 2008

The walls are shrinking around me
    And so am I
I am trapped within this place
    Within myself
And there is no way out
    Nowhere to go
Nothing to do
    To escape this mess I've gotten myself into

And so I let myself bleed
    I let myself overflow with tears
And I let myself be consumed
    By the darkness
By everything that surrounds me
    By every emotion
That is making me sink deeper into sorrow

I surrender myself
    I surrender my heart
To everything
    And everyone
And let the moment consume me
    Bit by bit
Until there is nothing left of me
    Not a speck of my existence
Not a speck of remembrance
    That I ever was
That I ever roamed this universe
    And that I ever will

~ I'M A MISTAKE ~
June 19, 2008

I'm a mistake
A big mistake
I wasn't supposed to be here
It was just an error
An error on their part
To bring me into this world
To cause me to suffer the way I did
Day by day
Night by night

If that mistake hadn't been made
Then I wouldn't be brought into this world
And I wouldn't be suffering
Day by day
Night by night
'Cause I would not be here

I wasn't supposed to be here in the first place
It was just an error
An error on their part
That brought me into this world

~ I'M NOT A DOG ~
June 19, 2008

You give me orders
Like I'm some dog on a leash
Someone you can control and boss around
Someone who will listen to you and obey your every command
Someone who is stupid enough to fall for your dirty scheme

Well, I am not stupid enough to fall for your dirty scheme
So I won't listen to you and obey your every command
I won't let you control me and boss me around
And I won't be taking your orders
'Cause I'm not a dog

A Crimson Tide | Poetry by Lena Kovadlo

~ I AM A RIVER ~
June 13, 2008

I
Am
A river
Cascading
Overflowing
From weary eyes
Sinking deep into pools
Of my torrential emotions
That seep through every pore
Every bit of my molecular flesh
And eat away the life that remains
Hidden inside of my still beating heart

Hidden inside of my still beating heart
And eating away the life that remains
Every bit of my molecular flesh
That seeps through every pore
Of my torrential emotions
Sinks deep into pools
From weary eyes
Overflowing
Cascading
A river
Am
I

A Crimson Tide | Poetry by Lena Kovadlo

About the Author:

When Lena Kovadlo puts pen to paper she spills out her heart and soul, never holding back, never being afraid to share it all with the world. Writing is her calling, her passion, and something she can't live without.

Ever since Lena mastered the English language, after moving to New York City at the age of nine from Minsk, Belarus, she began to write. Since then she has brought to life hundreds of poems and lyrics, as well as short stories, prose, fiction, and non-fiction pieces. She has also published six books, ***A Crimson Tide*** being her seventh book, which is quite an accomplishment for someone who came to this country with no knowledge of the English language except for the word *NO*.

With much success in the world of writing, she is proud to be the recipient of **Achievement in Poetry** and **Editor's Choice** awards and be a winner in various writing contests, among which are poetry and lyric contests... She has also won awards on writing.com. Her poetry has been published in anthologies by various publishers.

Besides writing, Lena enjoys singing, dancing, performing, cooking, reading, listening to music, going to concerts and shows, traveling, hiking, sports, and much more.

She currently lives in Staten Island, NY and is a freelance writer for HubPages.com.

To check out Lena's writing and learn more about her, her books, and her creative projects visit her website at: **http://lovebuglena.webs.com**

Dear Regis,

Thank you for always supporting me and my writing on AD, HubPages and beyond, for leaving your comments and for being a great fan and friend.

You are a very talented writer and poet. Much success to you with your books and your poetry and other writing. You rock!!!

Your friend
Lena Kovadlo
1/4/2013